Overcoming Your Devotional Obstacles

John O'Malley

to Kimberly, the one who makes my heart smile

CHAPTER ONE

INTRODUCTION

MY LETTER TO YOU

Dear Reader,

This book will take us on a path together. I hope you will be honest with yourself and with God as you read it. As you read this book, I would like you to know that your Devotions should not be a time of pressure or performance. Your time with God each day must become the moment where you pause your life and listen to God.

Our Quiet Time with God was never meant to be an item to check off from our things to do for the day. Our devotions were never intended to be something we did as a step in a formula to become Super Christians. Our Devotions are intended to be like the walk with God that Eve and Adam had in Eden. Our Quiet Time should be like Daniel's faithful prayer meeting at the window of his house or like Moses' meeting with God in the cleft of the rock.

There are three things I need you to remember as you read this book.

First, we need to remember that God is our Partner. God, through the Holy Spirit, breathed His words into men to write the Scriptures as He intended. When Jesus left the earth, He left us a Comforter and a Counselor in the person of His Holy Spirit. You are never alone when you read the Bible. If you are in a faith-relationship with Jesus Christ, He gave you the Holy Spirit to live with you. When you pick up your Bible to meet God, remember He resides in you. He is your Partner; you are not alone.

The second thing we need to remember is His promise. He said that He would never leave us nor forsake us (Hebrews 13:5). Our Quiet Time with Him is more about discovering His presence than finding the perfect Bible reading plan or study method. If we complete a Bible reading plan and did not discover His presence, we may have checked off the box for the day on our daily Bible reading plan, but we missed Him.

The third thing to remember is our relationship with God is based on His grace and not our performance. God is our Father. He wants to meet us in His Word. We have this eternal and amazing grace-based relationship with the Creator of the Universe. He knows our name and nature, and He loves us. He knows all of our inconsistencies, guilt issues, and life's dramas.

He works with us where we are.

Do you know what? God loves it when we show up with His Word in our hand and faith in our heart with the intention to listen and learn (Hebrews 11:6). Let us discover how you can meet Him today.

Your friend on the devotional journey,

John

WHY?

I wrote *Overcoming Your Devotional Obstacles* because people face obstacles as they read their Bible and devotional books, and have their Quiet Time with God.

Overcoming Your Devotional Obstacles confronts the obstacles people face when it comes to doing their Devotions. Other book titles might have been *Seven Reasons My Devotions Fail Me* or *Seven Reasons I Fail in My Devotions*. However, I did not allow this book to be called by those alternative titles.

The reason I cannot bring myself to call this book by those alternate titles is because I refuse to start with a limiting belief as I work through my devotional issues. A limiting belief is a belief that focuses on the reasons why I cannot overcome my obstacles; it then affects how I behave. I chose the title *Overcoming Your Devotional Obstacles* because it identifies and resolves the obstacles to our devotions. This book teaches how to overcome those difficulties with a positive outlook rather than establishing limiting beliefs or developing a culture of guilt by trying to make you feel sorry about your devotional life.

Try to avoid the temptation to blame yourself or someone else for your current position on why or how you are displeased with your Devotions. It is a great place to be when you can recognize the obstacles. It is not okay to become a victim and blame your pastor or Sunday School teacher for where you are in your devotional journey. Do not seek to assign blame to the person who led you to Jesus, who may have done a poor job on teaching you how to have Devotions. Assigning responsibility to someone else for your own devotional deficiency only traps you in a prison of your making. Release yourself from blaming others and own where you are.

Where are you right now on your spiritual journey? Let us agree to start here: you are a Christian who is not satisfied with your devotional life. Perhaps you share my desire to have Devotions that are meaningful and memorable. These are good things; this is a good place. We can begin together from here to overcome our common obstacles.

In this book, I will show you the common obstacles most people have with their devotional time. Then I will teach you how to overcome them. How you got to this place is not as important to me as how you are going to overcome the obstacles and have Devotions you can remember and apply.

My purposes for this book:

Overcoming Your Devotional Obstacles is not about assigning blame for whose fault it is that you do not have meaningful and memorable Devotions.

Overcoming Your Devotional Obstacles is about putting tools in your hand to help you go from defeated to victorious in your time alone with God.

Overcoming Your Devotional Obstacles is written to identify the common obstacles in your Devotions and help you overcome those barriers.

What are your obstacles to having memorable and meaningful devotions? Read this list and see if any of the obstacles resonate with you.

1. **The Obstacle of Distraction--***I read my Bible, but I get distracted and sometimes even lose interest in what I read.*

2. **The Obstacle of History--***I seem to miss the meaning of the passage I read. I think it is because I do not understand the background or history of the Bible.*

3. **The Obstacle of Comparison--***I feel inadequate, overwhelmed, or guilty when I hear others speak of a beautiful time of Devotions and I compare my devotions to theirs.*

4. **The Obstacle of Time--***I want to read it, but I just do not have enough time in my day to have memorable or meaningful*

Devotions.

5. **The Obstacle of Comprehension--***I just do not know how to get anything out of my Bible reading.*

6. **The Obstacle of Recollection--***I wish I could remember my Devotions thirty minutes later. I tried. I failed. It makes me feel the negative emotions of guilt and sadness.*

7. **The Obstacle of Application--***I do not know how to apply Scripture to my life.*

Is any of the above true in your life? I know at one time or another I lived with or helped someone with at least one of these scenarios. What you will read in this book is how to overcome these devotional obstacles. I believe a Bible reader can overcome the obstacles to their Devotions. I know they will work for you because they worked for me.

Here is my commitment to you: If you cannot find your way over the obstacles you face to having a meaningful and memorable devotional time, email me or call me with your struggle. I will pray with you and personally suggest what I would do to help you. My contact information is in the Bonus Section under Resources.

This book is designed to let you jump straight to your greatest obstacle. This book can be read straight through, or you can just read the sections that apply to you. Be sure to check the

Bonus Section for additional resources and an offer to get special and early access to what I am writing next.

WHAT?

What do you call your devotional time?

In this book, I will use specific terms to describe the single activity of meeting with God. The period of time we reserve to meet God is called many things. Some of the names sound majestic and poetic, while other names are quite dull. Perhaps you have a different name you prefer to call this meeting. If the name of what you call your time alone with God is not on the list, email and let me know what you call yours.

Some of the names I hear used to describe this meeting with God are:

- Devotions
- God and I Time
- Reservation With God
- Time Alone With God
- Quiet Time
- Prayer Time
- Bible Reading Time

- ◆ Reflection
- ◆ Vespers (if it is in the evening)

Collectively, these names portray images in my mind; I recognize a picture of the Creator meeting with His creation. I see an image of a Father with His child. I see a forgiven woman who is profoundly humbled to be in the presence of God; she sits with attentive posture and eyes that are moist with truthful tears. I imagine a quiet room with soft lighting, soft music, and a person seated with the word of God. I see a man who looks at the page of Scripture, yet he seems focused well beyond the pages. His eyes are fixed solely on the Author.

Sometimes those images can mess us up when it comes to comparing those scenes to our reality of having our Devotions. Instead of a peaceful setting, we have our homes, with real noises, real kids, and real messes. It seems impossible to find a spot to sit to meet with God without having to move a pet, person, or pile of clothes. If you could have the entire time set aside with God, it would be a miracle if you are not interrupted by a scream, spill, or sibling disaster.

Sadly, more often than not, our reality is we grab a verse and say, "God give me your best shot. I do not have much time today." We read the passage or verse and walk away with a void.

You say: "This is not how it is supposed to be, but here I am. How do I overcome my obstacles to having my time for reflection from God's Word? I need someone to help me. I need answers without guilt. I need solutions with substance. I wish someone would hold back the forces of interruption of my life, sit next to me, take my hand, and guide me on how to overcome my devotional obstacles. I want to have meaningful and memorable Devotions--not just for one day, but every day."

My purpose in writing *Overcoming Your Devotional Obstacles* is to help people in their Bible reading and Devotions. When I write devotional books, I do so to take people to the classroom of Bible learning to teach a Bible lesson. The individual lesson I teach shares either a principle, precept, or promise from within the passage. I am not content with just giving the reader a lesson and closing out the class.

The second part of my lesson is to take my reader from the Bible learning classroom on a field trip to a place called Bible Living. I do not want what I write to say, "Here is a truth. Figure it out." I take a simple element from life and show you how to live that Bible lesson outside the classroom. I write to bring my readers to the place where Bible learning and Bible living come together. When my reader sees that Bible living is what we do because of Bible learning, it is then we will use our lives to bring Him glory.

IS THIS YOUR LIFE?

Read these scenarios and see if you can identify with any of them.

Scenario One:

You are listening to your favorite Bible teacher or preacher. Perhaps you are listening while in your car, at church, at work, and you hear them say something of particular interest or mention a fact from Bible history. You can hear the audience seem to acknowledge audibly the words of the messenger. You know the feeling when you hear the speaker say, "Now we are all aware since Adam was Methuselah's grandfather, that means they knew each for over 240 years."

You sit there and say, "What did he just say? I have never heard that! How did he know that? How can everyone else in the room know this, and I just found this out? Look at the person over there! She has been in church half the time I have, and she knew that? What is wrong with me?"

It is easy to assign blame to formal education and how it was out of reach for you. You can say, "I went to secular university and not a Christian college, so that is why I do not know." You may dismiss this as something you must have missed that week in Sunday School.

These moments can be disheartening and even discouraging. *Overcoming Your Devotional Obstacles* is designed to help you if this is where you are.

See obstacles two, five, six and seven for more advice.

Scenario Two:

Our devotional time can be where a feeling of inadequacy arises more than at any other time. You read a passage of Scripture, and you look at it and say, "I do not understand that verse or principle! I thought it meant the opposite." Take for example the moment where you read David was a man after God's own heart, yet his home was so dysfunctional it makes your life seem somewhat normal. You read your devotional reading, and you know the meaning of the word in English, but you scratch your head saying, "What am I missing here?" You read about an event and wonder about its placement or significance. There is a pressure of inadequacy which comes from thinking you should know more than you do.

The ability to read and retain what you read is hard enough some days. So when it comes to taking what you just read and applying it to your life, you hit a wall and cannot get around it. So you respectfully close your Bible application or bound volume and close your eyes and say, "How am I supposed to live that verse? I do not even understand the history or background of what I read, no less, how on earth will I live it." When it comes to the application of a passage, it seems you never cross the goal line or finish the recipe. You just leave it and say, "I am not smart enough. I will ask someone who has a spiritual post today on Facebook or Instagram to see if they know."

It is okay to have moments when you do not understand how to apply a verse. For some it would be more appropriate to say, "It is not moments when I do not understand; it is rare that I do know how to apply a verse to my life!"

Perhaps another example is the moment where you read in the book of Judges, and you see a battle lost in a two-lettered town called Ai. You may wonder, "How do I apply the death of thirty-six faithful men to my life when I just want to know how to help my child become potty-trained?"

Learning how to apply the Bible to one's life does not require formal education, a pastor on retainer, or thousands of dollars in books. Applying the Bible is a learned practice.

See Obstacles one, five, six, and seven for more advice.

CHAPTER TWO

THE OBSTACLE OF DISTRACTION

THE OBSTACLE OF DISTRACTION

The Obstacle of Distraction--*I read my Bible, but I get distracted and sometimes even lose interest in what I read.*

Our hearts and minds are bombarded with thousands of messages each day. These messages come from our technology, our work, our children, our academic institutions, our churches, our medical professionals, and our spouse. Those messages are just from the relationships in our lives.

Then we get to the advertisers who spend millions of dollars each year to get us to remember the name of their product when that particular need arises in our lives. We look at our televisions; then we listen to the radio and podcasts. Everyone has a message for us to recall. The message we hear and see is "Buy this; do this; face this; go here or there; lose weight and exercise." Do not forget how wonderful your life would be if their product were a daily part of your life! On your way to work, there are messages on billboards, magazines, and books. You check your phone, Twitter, Facebook, Snapchat, and

Instagram accounts, and discover even more messages to process.

The messages that find us each day are not always wrong. Sometimes the words we read bring good news, and others messages we read do not bring good news. These inbound messages seem to assault us the moment we wake up in the morning until we are lying in bed in the glow of our phones. In a world filled with messages from technology, relationships, and society's advertisers, what makes those slogans, jingles, and images stick in our mind?

Why is it we go to church and by the time we get to the meal after service, we cannot remember the sermon or even think of the Small Group, Bible Study, or Sunday School lesson? Why is it we can remember the jingle from a fast-food restaurant from two decades ago, but we cannot remember what the Lord showed us that day in His Word?

This devotional obstacle of distraction is common, real, and embarrassing. How do I have meaningful and memorable Devotions when I so easily lose interest or am so easily distracted?

Tip #1: Create an environment of solitude.

What are the hours you are the most alert during the day?

Do you function best in the morning, afternoon, evening, or after 9:00 p.m.? In those hours when you are at your prime, can you create an environment of solitude for ten to fifteen minutes? Perhaps you will need to go outside or use headphones to play instrumental music. Maybe you need to designate a special signal for your family that this is your time to connect with God. Maybe it is a closet, garage, shed, or bathroom. You need to create the environment where you can hear God's Word and listen to His leading.

Tip #2: Choose one or two verses from that day's Bible reading on which you will mediate.

I never do well keeping my interest when I am trying to swallow an entire chapter. When I need to work on keeping interest and focus, I settle on one or two verses. I then take advantage of the Bible study methods in the resource section and begin to work through that passage. If you are using a devotional book that has a Scripture portion, a short section of inspiration or instruction, and a brief application, use that Scripture portion. Take a 3x5 card and write the verse on the card. Write it neatly and deliberately, and add the punctuation marks. Meditate as you write the words. Sometimes I imagine I am a scribe copying the Word of God from parchment to parchment. It helps me focus and keep interest.

Tip #3: Write down three thoughts about the passage.

Take the same 3x5 card and turn it over. Write down these three words: *Inspires. Instructs. Includes.*

Look at the verse you wrote. What inspires you in this passage? Is there a phrase that makes you want to praise or pray? Is there a thought or a moment in that verse that moves you? Is there a promise in this verse that comforts you? Write the thought that inspires you by the first word you wrote: *Inspires.*

Now, look at the next word: *Instructs.* What precept or principle is mentioned in this verse that teaches or is an instruction for you? Is there a truth in this verse that reminds you of a problem you are facing? Look further. Think about it for a moment. Is there instruction in this passage for a problem you are facing today? Is there a principle that you see in this passage to apply to your life today? Although we may not see a principle for today, it may be a principle we need for tomorrow! We can see how God typically works to help us when we face that in the future. What instructs you in this verse? Write what you see as God's instruction for you by the word you wrote earlier: *Instructs.*

Now look at the third word: *Includes.* Look at the verse

OVERCOMING YOUR DEVOTIONAL OBSTACLES

again on the front side of your card. Read the verse aloud and listen to how your name could be included in the place of the names or pronouns mentioned in the verse. (*See the example below.*) Look for how you are included in the promise, principle, precept, proclamation, or prohibition in that verse. Now, write one sentence beside the word *Includes:* You could start it with *This verse includes me because...* or *I am included in this verse because...*

Example of Using the 3x5 Bible Study Method
My verse: *"For by grace are ye saved through faith; and that not of yourselves: it is the gift of God:"* (Ephesians 2:8).

Inspires: The truth that my salvation is by grace **inspires** me.

Instructs: I am **instructed** that salvation is a gift, not a work.

Includes: I am **included** in salvation because of God's gift of grace.

Now, read aloud from both sides of the card. This next step is very important. I want you to take that card with you for the next twenty-four hours and set an appointment on your phone to read it over at least four times in the next twenty-four hours. If you prefer a nighttime Devotions, then read it before you go to bed, when you get up in the morning, when you have lunch, and then again when you have supper.

My goal is to give you a tool to overcome the **Obstacle of Distraction**. You can do this Bible study method. This 3x5 card method keeps you interested and distraction-free because anyone can fill out a 3x5 card with ease.

If you used this method and it helped, email me to let me know. My email address is also in the Bonus Section.

CHAPTER THREE

THE OBSTACLE OF HISTORY

THE OBSTACLE OF HISTORY

The Obstacle of History--*I seem to miss the meaning of the passage I read. I think it is because I do not understand the background or history of the Bible.*

Have you ever been to a family event with someone who was new to the family? Maybe they just married into the family, or they are getting acquainted with one of the family members. They get the speech, "Do not ask Cousin Eddy about his toupee. Do not ask Aunt Loo-dell how she is feeling."

You share this with your guest because you know the background of the family. You know the history of your relatives. You know what occurs when people ask specific questions about particular people in front of them.

The family event is underway. Your guest is asking you questions to learn about the family's history and the relationships between the different people they meet. You find yourself as a teacher helping your one student in the classroom of your family.

In a sense, you are a guide; you are walking your friend through the museum of your family. Then when it comes to relatives where there is an air of tension, you find yourself an adviser who comes alongside your guest and whispers the right word or phrase to help them through a moment of difficulty.

Your Quiet Time with God can be this way. You walk through the annals of history preserved for us by God. On each page of Scripture, there is a context and culture. Each passage occurs in a context of family dynamics, tensions, and complex relationships. Each chapter takes place in a period that may be difficult to make a modern-day connection.

You hold in your hands the greatest Book ever written. You know it contains a message for you. However, you look at the verses like your guest did at the family event. You whisper, "Can you help me here? I need to understand something."

You know you have been in the same position. You look at the verse carefully and you know the words' meanings for the most part. You see the names of people that are familiar but do not know the family dynamics. You see in the verse there are cultural markers that have significance, but you grew up in a different place and time, so you are a little stuck. You even sense some tension in the passage, but you cannot figure out the significance. Like your friend at a family event, you need a guide, an advisor, and a family teacher to help.

It gets harder when you read a verse that has no people, no places, no cultural marker, or no family dynamics. You are looking at a principle or Bible doctrine--a set of teachings and beliefs held by people of faith. You ponder the verse and say, "What am I to do about this?"

You think, "I just need a mashup of Wikipedia and Google but just for the Bible. If I could just put in a search phrase to get an immediate answer." I have tried that, but it does not work that readily. Then you get other information that you did not even realize existed, and ten minutes later you still know nothing.

These feelings about Bible reading are real. I have felt all of them. When I feel that way, I try to remind myself that I am like the person at the family reunion. I see something I do not grasp. I need to understand. I need a personal teacher, a guide, and counselor. I need someone who has been in this family a long time to advise me. I know a specific passage or verse is not intended to be hard. I need someone who will help me understand the sense of the passage. It is at times like these I have said, "If someone sat beside me as I read and helped me understand the sense, I would not feel like the dumbest person in the room (even if I am alone)."

God did not hand us His Word and say, "Here, you figure it out." God gave us better than a Google/Wikipedia mash-up for the Bible. God gave us a Guide, Teacher, Counselor, and Adviser to go along with His Word. He dwells within the heart of the child of God. You may say, "I know the Holy Spirit lives within me, but I want to ask questions and get answers, immediately."

Having a Quiet Time with God should not leave you feeling dumb when you cannot get the sense of the passage because you do not know the history or background. The Bible is not intended to make you feel inadequate because you do not have a post-graduate degree in ancient culture, language, and history. It is possible to know the history or background of the Bible.

Consider this, the One who exhaled the Scriptures into those who held a pen for God also sent you the Holy Spirit to teach you. That means you can ask the Resident Guide who lives within you. Each time you read the Bible, you are stepping into a family event. You need someone to whisper in your ear about what has happened before this event and what is going on now in light of past events. If the One, who inspired the Word of God, lives within you, you will always have a Counselor.

Agreeing to the truth that the Holy Spirit lives within you, how do you get the answers from Him? For me, it begins with prayer. Let me tell you what I say. "God, I know there are things here I am not getting. I need your Holy Spirit to teach me this. Please guide me."

Sometimes, my answer has come shortly after that as I continued to read the verses before it and after it. I have also had my answers come months later when I read the verse again. Other times, I will read a similar thought in another passage and realize that is what the passage I got stuck on meant.

Your premise, when you begin any study of a passage, should be that the Bible is God's Word and is the answer to every human need; it is inerrant and infallible. Remember, the passage is about real people in a real place with real needs. You know as a fact that there is something in this passage God included for you to know. (The Bible is very personal that way.) God did not put random words in the passage to confuse me. He put it there to help me.

I believe God has enabled believers in every generation to explain the sense of a text. (See Nehemiah 8:8). There are excellent resources available to help with Bible backgrounds. I will include links to them in the resource section of this book.

What should you do to overcome the feeling that you do not

understand the background and history of a passage?

1.   Pray: "God, I know there are things here I am not understanding. I need your Holy Spirit to teach me this. Please guide me."

2.   Pick a resource: It can be online, digital eBook, or bound.

3.   Ask your pastor or Sunday School teacher: "Is there something in the background of this passage that would help me understand this section?"

You can know the background and history of a passage. I refuse to let an obstacle get in the way of me understanding what God wants me to know.

Tip #1: Remember the culture.

Culture is the system of beliefs, values, and ideas of a people in a certain time period. When you read the Bible, there was a definite culture. It is not a Western culture; it is an Eastern culture. The values of Western culture see things from a right and wrong perspective. Eastern culture will often times see things through a prism of what brings shame and what restores honor. When you read the Old Testament, you have to understand that your way of thinking cannot be projected onto their way of thinking. Furthermore, the culture of Heaven and the mind of God far outstrips any of our understanding. God and His Word are transcultural. You will be able to understand what is happening when you enter the cultural mindset of the people about whom you are reading.

Tip #2: Remember the context.

Learn to read the Bible by paragraph not just the numbered verses. This is critical in understanding the verses you are reading. You will become frustrated quickly if you isolate a verse from its context and try to bend it to what you want it to say or not say. If you ignore the context, you will miss the meaning and teaching. Reading the Bible by paragraph helps correct this. Get a good Bible that marks the paragraphs clearly or is printed in paragraphs. You will find a link for this in the Bonus Section under resources. I always encourage people to read it grammatically or like they would read a book. If the numbers are getting in the way, get a Bible that does not have them, so that when you read Paul's letters, they read like real letters! Check the Bonus Section for the Bible I use for reading passages by paragraph.

Tip #3: Remember the conflicts.

The sin nature of man is in conflict with the righteousness of God. You will find man's will takes him beyond the will and righteousness of God. Many of the accounts in Scripture describe when man's will dominates and God brings man to a place of correction and contrition. Contrition is a Bible word that gives the sense of being crushed or humbled. God values when our hearts and spirits are contrite. When you read a passage and the culture is so different and the context is not easily grasped, remember that man's will and desire is selfish. God will correct those who are wrong. He will forgive and restore those who confess their sin. Remember, before you boast that you might be better than another, you are a sinner saved by grace like those in the passage you are studying. Stay close to Him. Keep your heart and spirit contrite.

Tip #4: Remember your Companion.

Just before Jesus went to the cross, He told His disciples that He would leave them, but He would not leave them comfortless. He would send them a Comforter (John 14:16). One of the Comforter's tasks is to bring all things to our remembrance. He dwells within us and guides us to truth. When I am stuck on a verse or passage of Scripture, I pray. I ask the Holy Spirit to guide me and help me to see or recall what I am not seeing. There have been times I have been stuck on a passage of Scripture for more than a year. Then one day I am reading in another section, and the Holy Spirit brings to mind what I was stuck on and shows me the connection. It is a wonderful thing to have the Holy Spirit turn the lights on in your mind.

My goal is to give you a tool to overcome the **Obstacle of**

History, the feeling like you miss the meaning because you do not understand the background or history of the Bible. When you get stuck, review these four tips. If you used this method and it helped, <u>email me</u> to let me know. My <u>email</u> address is in the Bonus Section.

CHAPTER FOUR

THE OBSTACLE OF COMPARISON

THE OBSTACLE OF COMPARISON

The Obstacle of Comparison--*I feel inadequate, overwhelmed, or guilty when I hear others speak of a beautiful time of Devotions and I compare my Devotions to theirs.*

Have you ever felt overwhelmed, guilty, or inadequate about your devotional life? You know the feeling.

You look at these picture perfect people with a mystical aura about them. You see their Instagram accounts and wonder why your Devotions do not have their glamour. Their social media accounts have photos with the perfect compositions. They place their coffee cup just right, a pen is near their notebook and set at the perfect angle. Their Bible is open to the right passage and marked with the appropriate highlighter. They have a hashtag that is perfect. They choose the perfect photo filter to make it look spiritual.

You look up from your screen and glance around your home. You see the ever-growing-and-always-insurmountable Mount

Laundry on the couch. You see a pile of dishes that are unwashed from yesterday's lunch. You look at your child and realize he or she did not change their clothes from yesterday; then again, neither did you. You look again at your friend's social media account and then look at your life. You feel guilty and overwhelmed. You feel like quitting because you can never match up to their picture-perfect devotional life.

Perhaps your life is similar to the one described above. Maybe you know it too well. You see the social media accounts of these picture-perfect people and wonder where do they live? Do they live in a spiritual bubble while you are stuck in a spiritual desert?

When it comes to your devotional life, you wonder...

...am I the only one who struggles with my devotional life?

...am I the only one who feels my entire prayer life is the time spent asking God to bless my bowl of Froot Loops at breakfast?

...am I the only one who reads the inspirational quotes on Instagram and calls it devotions?

Do you have an empty spirit and a dry soul?

You wake up and try to motivate your family to leave on time. You grab your morning beverage and your Bible.

Thoughts rush through your mind as you sit down to read. You try to focus, but you cannot. There are more tasks than there is day. You grab the daily devotional to see a passage to read. It is not as though you are reading; it is more like you are scanning the words.

You pray, "God let my mind be something more than Teflon today. Please let something stick in my heart." You realize how empty your spirit is and dry your soul has become. You whisper a prayer and glance at your social media, hoping someone posts something inspirational so you can feel spiritual enough to take on the day.

Do you feel inadequate, overwhelmed, and guilty?

You rush to leave for work, and you know you will see your co-worker who is a believer. They will look perfect and have just the right thing to say. You get the feeling they spent hours with God before sunrise and sang hymns on the way to work. You look within and wonder, "What do they have that I do not have? Where do they get the time to do their devotions? I see them and feel guilty, overwhelmed, and inadequate."

On your drive into work, you struggle with guilt that comes from comparing yourself to others. Then you have to process these feelings of inadequacy. How can you get past these feelings of spiritual inadequacy? You get the sense of being overwhelmed in your spiritual life.

Does life interfere with your walk with God?

The kids are still asleep, the coffee or tea is excellent, your spouse is in their personal space, and you open the Bible. You forgot the last time you read it. So, you decide, you will use the tried and true flop and plop Bible reading method. Flop the Bible open, plop your finger down, and start reading. You read for ten minutes, and you think, "What did I just read?" So you read it again.

Finally, you just bow your head and say, "God, I read your Word today. Please help me understand it and even remember it." The next moment life explodes and your hectic day and life begins again.

The next thing you know, it is ten hours later and you have everyone fed, bathed, and in bed. You sit down to breath, and you see your Bible where you left it just before the morning exploded.

You close your eyes, take a deep spiritual breath, and you realize just how much life interferes with everything you do to have a closer walk with the Lord.

Why does it have to be this way?

How can I get to the picture-perfect devotional life?

How can I live this life and be close to Him?

How can I get to the place where I feel like I spent time with God, and it was meaningful to me and memorable throughout the day that I was with God?

Here are some tips to help you overcome the obstacles of guilt, inadequacy, and feeling overwhelmed by the quality of your Devotions.

Tip #1: Release yourself.

You must not trap yourself when viewing devotional posts on social media, nor when hearing people speak of their spiritual lives in a way that makes you feel guilty. The posts you see, including the inspirational quotes, capture a planned moment, not a perfect life. The way you imagine the picture of someone else's life from what they portray is unfair to you both. Life is messy--even for the believer.

The perfect people you see in a photo are not really perfect. Your fellow humans are as troubled as you are in your life. They have family problems mixed with financial problems. They have relationship issues and real struggles. We hurt ourselves when we compare ourselves to others without taking this into account.

Look at this passage:

> *"For we dare not make ourselves of the number, or compare ourselves with some that commend themselves: but they measuring themselves by themselves, and comparing themselves among themselves, are not wise"* (2 Corinthians 10:12).

There is a danger when we compare ourselves to each other. When you look at someone's photos and quotes, you are setting the expectation and creating your guilt, inadequacy, and sense of being overwhelmed. These unrealistic expectations get us out of balance, and we end up binding ourselves to unrealistic standards.

We are not wise when we begin comparing our lives with someone else's life. We are foolish when we measure our lives by another's life. Release yourself from such bondage; we are all sinners are saved by grace.

If you have a great moment in your life, take a mental or actual picture and enjoy it. If someone else has a great moment, rejoice equally. The next photo you see that makes you feel inadequate, remind yourself that picture is the image of a time when life was the way the photographer wanted to capture it.

We look idyllically at one another's lives and have no idea how difficult their lives are. Paul's admonition to the church at Ephesus in Ephesians 5:18 is to walk circumspectly. The words *"walk circumspectly"* mean we should live accurately (to who we are as a believer and whose we are, God's) and carefully (do not fall into the traps of this life or the trap of envy and pride).

Allow yourself to take a picture of when life gets messy. Release yourself from other people's picture frames and live in the picture frame of His grace and mercy.

Tip #2: Remind yourself.

When next you begin to evaluate and compare yourself to someone, remind yourself of your worth to God *(1 Corinthians 6:20)*. Tell yourself He paid far too high a price for you to create your storm of inadequacy, which leaves you overwhelmed. Your worth to God is unparalleled and priceless. God valued your worth to Him at such a high price that the only equivalent value was the death of His Son, Jesus. He gave His Son so that you could have fellowship with Him *(John 3:16)*.

Remind yourself of your worth to God in the roles you have

in life. You have a role as a wife, husband, and/or child of your parents. No matter your role, your value to Him is unsurpassed. Your worth to God as a woman is far above rubies (Genesis 2:18; Proverbs 31:10). Your worth to God as a husband is so great that He entrusted you to guard and guide those within your care *(Ephesians 5:23-25)*. Your worth as a teen (1 Samuel 16:11-12; Esther 2:7-11; 4:14) is not how you see yourself, or even as others see you; it is how He sees you.

Remind yourself of all the things that do not make it into the testimony you are pondering. They skipped the parts where they were alone and cried. They leapt over the parts where they did not have the strength to go on. They omitted the part where it took everything they had to find the bright parts to share in public (Philippians 3:13; 4:8).

Remind yourself that the photographer cropped the photo. There are things left out of the picture that you did not see or hear. While we do not see what is cropped out, believe me, it is there. It is not what the lens captures that matters in life, but what is important is what your mind captures from God's Word and what you hide from it in your heart (Colossians 3:1-4).

Remind yourself the next time you begin to envy or brood

over a whisper heard, an image you saw, or a perception you imagined, that person has as many, if not more, insecurities than you have. When feeling overwhelmed with all the perfect testimonies and images, pray for calmness in your spirit. When feeling guilty about what someone portrays and what you think you lack, pray for contentment in your soul (Philippians 4:11; 1 Timothy 6:6-8).

Tip #3: Reset yourself.

When feeling the sense of inadequacy about yourself, when feeling guilt about your walk with God, when feeling overwhelmed because everyone but you seems to have a perfect life, stop it! Be realistic and reset your expectations from the Word of God.

We reset our phones, our computers, and our cars. We also need to do this with our lives, and at times with our relationships and responsibilities. We must do this often with our thinking.

The only way I know to reset myself is time spent in the Word of God. I have to get back to the Bible and read it to reset my expectations about my walk with God, my prayer time, and my daily reading.

The Psalmist wrote in Psalm 42:5:

"Why art thou cast down, O my soul? and why art thou disquieted in me? hope thou in God: for I shall yet praise him for the help of his countenance."

The Psalmist made it clear: there is no valid reason to have noisiness (disquiet) in our souls. When our minds manufacture the noisiness of guilt, inadequacy, and the feeling of being overwhelmed, we must reset our thoughts with this thought, "I must hope in God and His presence (countenance)." No one has ever accurately said God failed him or her, and you cannot say God has failed you. Noisiness in the soul is a choice of the mind. Hope is a choice you must make when disquiet invades you.

When the disquietness comes within, press the Spiritual Reset Button of your spiritual life. Pressing the Spiritual Reset Button changes at least three things in you. These three things are realistic expectations to have concerning your Quiet Time with God. In the Bonus Section, I give you a full explanation on how to press the Spiritual Reset Button.

Reset the expectation of your walk with God.

What does your walk with God mean? It is your journey with the Creator of the Universe on the path of your life. Your stride, your view, and your memories will be different than someone else who reads the same passages you do. Like a parent individually teaches each child, the Holy Spirit impresses each reader in the way they need to hear and learn.

Why then would you compare your Bible journey to someone else's Bible journey? You will have a different stride, a different view, and a different experience than someone else. You must reset your thinking about comparing your devotional life with anyone else. You must begin to ask, "God, am I meeting Your expectations in my walk with You?"

Reset the expectations about the time you pray.

Pressing the Spiritual Reset Button on prayer helps you determine what level of prayer life you should have. The comparison between another's prayer life and your own will either make you feel pride or pity. Neither emotion is an accurate metric to assess whether you pray enough or if you pray as long or just like someone else. Do you recall what occurred in the temple in Luke 18:9-14? The Pharisee and the Publican both prayed to God, but their hearts were different. What is your heart filled with when you pray?

When you choose to press the Spiritual Reset Button, your prayer life changes, ending the childish comparison with others. Prayer is talking to God about what is in your heart and listening to Him speak through His Word. Do not complicate prayer. Do not compare your prayer time with another. Doing so cheapens your intimate conversations with God and diminishes you.

In the Bonus Section you will find the books on prayer and Christian growth which I enjoy.

Reset the expectations about your Bible reading.

What does life look like after you press the Spiritual Reset Button? Let your Bible reading be more about what you retain and live out versus how much you read and left out of your life. I recommend you start with quality over quantity. If you are using a devotional book, take the passage for the day and read it. Read it slowly and deliberately. Read it aloud, perhaps even listen to it being read with an audio Bible. Now, read the day's reading of inspiration or instruction. Did the passage from the Bible or the day's reading resonate with you? Is there an area of your life you need to make it apply?

If you are prone to comparing your Bible reading and devotional reading time with someone, stop it. It is not healthy for your spiritual life. It will leave you overwhelmed, guilty, and feeling less than adequate.

Tip #4: Fill out a 3x5 card and carry it with you.

Fill out this card as instructed below. Put it in your wallet, save it on your phone or tablet, put it in your purse so you can pull it out and review it when you feel the emotions of inadequacy, guilt, and being overwhelmed when you have reverted to comparisons.

1. Write this statement across the top of the card. Write this verse below it.

Statement: I will not compare myself to others in any area of my life. It is not wise.

Verse: *"For we dare not make ourselves of the number, or compare ourselves with some that commend themselves: but they measuring themselves by themselves, and comparing themselves among themselves, are not wise"* (2 Corinthians 10:12).

2. Turn the card over and write this statement across the top and this verse below it.

Statement: I will choose hope and praise over the

noisiness of my emotions. Any other choice will frustrate me.

Verse: *"Why art thou cast down, O my soul? and why art thou disquieted in me? Hope thou in God: for I shall yet praise him For the help of his countenance"* (Psalm 42:5).

3. In the Bonus Section, there will be a link to download a graphic for your phone and to print out your own copy.

My goal is to give you a tool to overcome the **Obstacle of Comparison.** You know the feelings of inadequacy, guilt, and being overwhelmed when you compare yourself to the spirituality of others. When you get stuck, review these four tips. If you used this method and it helped, email me to let me know. My email address is in the Bonus Section.

CHAPTER FIVE

THE OBSTACLE OF TIME

THE OBSTACLE OF TIME

The Obstacle of Time--*I want to read it, but I just do not have enough time in my day to have memorable or meaningful Devotions.*

The more I speak to others about their time alone with God, the more I learn I am not alone. Many of us struggle with making time for God; we tell ourselves we do not have enough time. We make excuses. We justify why we have not done it. We give our time to the right things and necessary things; we surrender to our schedules and obligations. We often cannot find a way to fit God into our day. We hate it, but it is the reality of most days.

We cannot add time to our lives. We have what is the time allotted for this vapor of a life. We use phrases like, "I need to make the time. I wish I had the time; I did not spend my time on this; or time is not my friend today." However, we know all of them are expressions spoken out of frustration.

When we say we do not have enough time in the day to have a

Quiet Time with God, how much time should we reserve for Him? The often thought yet unspoken sentiments say, "How much time is 'enough' to say I did my Devotions? How long do I need to give Him? How much time should we plan on spending with God for a meaningful experience?" We will say to justify our heart's emotion, "I have things I have to do. I do not have a lot of time just to sit still. I have kids, tasks, appointments, and obligations that are calling me."

How is it that we willingly schedule appointments in our lives for everything that meets an emotional need in our lives? We schedule time for work because we trade our life's hours for dollars. We schedule time for play because we sell our time for momentary happiness. We plan time for the academic institutions in our lives because we exchange time for academic credentials. We plan time for the church because we are willing to trade our time for fellowship and ministry.

The Psalmist said in Psalm sixty-three, he sought God early in the day. He pointed to the human condition of hungering and thirsting to be with God. He speaks of how his vision, praise, and memories are affected when he spent time with God. He spoke of how his rest was directly related to his spending time with God.

When we do not spend time with God, we deplete ourselves.

54

We deplete our peace, joy, and strength. When limiting our access to time with God, we tend to lean on our own understanding; we are filled with doubts, and we consult our own heart instead of the mind of God (Proverbs 3:5-6).

When it comes to our personal time with God, we allow other things to intercept our time. We feel sorry for it, yet it happens. We want to do better with it, but we still let it happen. Why? I believe it is not about wishing, wanting, having, or making more time. It is about making a reservation in your day to meet God.

Making a reservation to meet God is about assigning a specific time to your day. It is about making no to everything that cries out for your day. It is about saying God the most important relationship in your life and treating Him as such. Scheduling time with God is not on His schedule. It is about your schedule. If you are going to have a meaningful time with God you must:

1.   Determine your best time of day--a time when you are not distracted by the day. The Psalmist David said he sought the Lord early in the day. You know your schedule and your best time.

2.   Make an appointment with God--a time not shared with anything or anyone else. Consider the appointment as exclusive access to the Creator of the

OVERCOMING YOUR DEVOTIONAL OBSTACLES

universe.

3.   Reserve time for reflection--a time where you process and assimilate what you read. It is not enough to accomplish a chapter reading or time spent reading without reflection. Reflection implies there is a certain glow or image that the Word of God casts on us. If I do not take time for reflection on my reading, I am just checking off a box on my things to do list.

4.   Reserve time to listen--the Bible is God's letter to us.   Read to hear the voice of the Author. Learn to understand the tone of His voice. Learn to listen to the message of the words. Jesus said that His sheep know, hear, and follow His voice. Your time with the Lord is about listening. God's Word is the answer to every human need. Read not to accomplish book or chapter count. Read and listen.

5.   Reserve time to speak with Him--at the end of your reservation with Him, share with Him your heart's difficulties and desires. He calls us to come to Him when we are weak; He urges us to pour out our hearts to Him.

Right now, look at tomorrow's schedule. What is more important than meeting God? Now, make a reservation with yourself to have time alone with God. Yes, a reservation.

How much time will you need? Schedule ten minutes where

you will shut the world out and sit with God and listen to Him. You may have to go outside. You may need to sit in your car. You may need to close a door. Do what it takes to make a reservation to meet Him.

We will discuss how to have meaningful time with God in another section. For simplicity's sake, here are some simple guidelines.

1.   Read one passage of Scripture. Start with a Psalm; look for His reflection in that passage.

2.   As you read the verses, remember you may need to read it several times to hear His voice and get a sense of the message of His words.

3.   Pause in prayerful reflection and say, "God, this is what I hear in your passage. Is there more you want me to see, learn, or know?"

Reserving ten minutes with God will change your day, your heart, and your outlook. Then in the following weeks, as you are comfortable doing so, increase the time you reserve with Him to fifteen minutes each day. There not a Biblical standard for minutes spent with Him. I am suggesting a ten-minute reservation with God to get you started.

You will not want to miss what He has planned for you

tomorrow in His Word. It will change your life.

Meet Him early. Meet Him often. Meet Him regularly. There is no substitute with your daily reservation with God.

Tip #1: Get your calendar out and set an appointment with God every day for the next thirty days.

I have my time set on my calendar. I have the reminder come up which forces me to click yes (I did it), no (I did not do it), or I can defer it for an hour from now. Use your phone, computer, tablet, or daily paper planner to do so. Do this today. Look at every other appointment you make in life. You set appointments for doctors, sports, and school. Make one with God on your calendar and keep it. Next month, clear your schedule again for a daily appointment with God.

If you set an appointment with God on your calendar for the next thirty days, <u>email</u> me to let me know. My <u>email</u> address is in the Bonus Section.

Tip #2: Take a simple inventory of where you spend your time.

How many hours do you sleep?

How many hours do you work each day?

How many hours do you spend in exercise?

How many hours do you spend in leisure?

How many minutes do you spend with God?

Consider how much time you should spend with God this week. Next month, evaluate yourself again. Set a goal to spend ten percent more time with God than you did last month.

This worksheet is in the Bonus Section.

Tip #3: Take a 3x5 card and add this to it:

Write this across the top. I spent _____ minutes with God today, and He taught me _____. (Then complete the statement.)

Carry that card with you during the day. Refer to it at meals and at bedtime. If your family has a conversation at a meal, then use this card to speak about what God taught you today to reinforce it. Encourage your spouse to do it on another night. Teach your children to do this also. This can bring a spiritual tone to your mealtimes.

Tip #4: Look in the Bonus Section for a Bible study tool or short reading plan to try for one week. The Bonus Section contains several Bible study methods and simple reading plans.

My goal is to give you a tool to overcome **the Obstacle of**

Time. When you get stuck, review these four tips. If you used this method, and it helped, <u>email</u> me to let me know. My <u>email</u> address is in the Bonus Section.

CHAPTER SIX
THE OBSTACLE OF
COMPREHENSION

THE OBSTACLE OF

COMPREHENSION

The Obstacle of Comprehension--*I just do not know how to get anything out of my Bible reading.*

In 1995, I was sitting in a restaurant in Dubai in the United Arab Emirates. I was traveling alone and knew not a single word in Arabic. What happened that day taught me a lesson about a common difficulty for Christians when it comes to their reservation with God each day.

It was time for breakfast, and I went into the restaurant. I smiled and realized I had just stepped into a restaurant with no English speakers. The server handed me a menu. I saw words and punctuation, but I did not comprehend a thing. The numbers were clearly Arabic, but recognizable. After doing an exchange rate in my head, I chose something in the middle price range.

I needed to communicate with the server, so I resorted to gestures, pointing, and mimicking cracking eggs over a bowl and scrambling them. The server pointed to something on the menu. I nodded yes, and he left for the kitchen. At that moment, I realized the value of learning languages, the benefit of understanding culture, and how smoothly things go when you know what you are doing. In my travels, I have ordered in restaurants in a non-English setting and gotten by without too many surprises. However, this day was one for the travel log and books.

The server returned smiling. I smiled back and whispered a prayer. He brought coffee and a sheep cheese and onion omelet. I received the breakfast and returned thanks to God. I would have ordered something different had I known the language, or brought a phrase book with me, or even had data access (which in Dubai in 1995 was nonexistent).

The breakfast was not terrible. It was an experience that taught me something about devotions. You can be in a familiar setting (a restaurant) and see visible markers (tables, chairs, servers, and food) and still be a bit lost and in need of a guide.

When it comes to your Bible reading and devotional time, you may be like I was in the restaurant. You get to the moment where you will meet God for the day. You open and read your

Bible, and suddenly you are seeing a familiar setting (Bible open) with clear markers (books of the Bible, chapters, and verses). However, the moment you start to read the words, you realize you do not understand what is happening in the passage. It is as if you are not getting the sense of the passage, and you wonder if it is the sheep cheese and onion omelet or something indescribable! Seriously speaking, when you finish reading your assigned Bible reading, you walk away without getting anything out of your time with God's Word. It is frustrating when this happens, butBible reading and Devotions do not have to be this way. This scenario is not what the experience is supposed to be for the believer.

After all, look at our friend's social media posts. They have crisp images and great quotes. You look at yourself and say, how do they get anything like that out of their readings? You hear their testimonies in Sunday School, Small Groups, or Bible Study. You know you have as much sense as they have, but why do you we feel this way? Why do you not understand or get anything out of your appointment with God?

When I am in a place of not knowing or getting anything out of my reservation with God, I know it is not Him. I know it is not His Word. So I feel guilty that I am not getting anything out of the Bible. Here I am a preacher, and sometimes even I feel that way.

The tips below to **Overcome the Obstacle of Comprehension** are what I use when I feel like I am not understanding or getting anything from my time in the Word of God.

Tip #1: Write these statements on a 3x5 card.

Put the card in your Bible or near your devotional book. Copy the words to your reading device and read them aloud before and after your quiet time.

I read the Bible to feel better, not worse.

I read the Bible to grow in grace, not in guilt.

I read the Bible to get to know the Author.

I read the Bible to become who God needs me to be for His glory.

I read the Bible not to impress others.

I read the Bible for God to make an impression on me.

Tip #2: Rest before reading.

The days I feel this way I look at my sleep schedule and consider, did I prepare for my reservation with God this morning by getting proper rest? As kids our parents would say to us, "Get some rest! Tomorrow is a big day." For the believer, each tomorrow is a big day. Each day I have a reservation with God. I will meet Him; He will speak to me, and I will talk to Him.

I know for many it is easy to recommend waking up earlier. That is fine if you are a morning person. Sometimes I feel like my "later at night" and my "earlier in the morning" will meet and there will be no more sleep.

You may be in a season of unrest. Your nights are filled with restlessness and thoughts of what might be coming next in your life. God works third shift. He never sleeps.

There have been many nights when I prayed the following based on thoughts of Psalm 127:

Dear Lord,

Your Word tells me you give Your children sleep. I know I am Your child. Please help my mind and body to get in sync to get some sleep. Will You please grant me sleep?

Until sleep comes, lay upon my heart someone for whom I should be praying right now.

Lord, if You chose to awake me at this hour to have me listen to You from Your Word, please speak to my heart.

Help me to have the strength I need for tomorrow.

Amen.

Tip #3: Remove distractions before reading.

My preferred way to read is to have headphones on with either ocean sounds or Baroque period music playing, or instrumental only music. (Check the Bonus Section for links to what I listen to while I am having my reservation with God.) I do not listen to music with words during this time. The music is softly playing.

Secure a space that will allow you a moment of privacy. I know many young mothers who retreat to private areas in the home to do their Bible reading. Seek your spouse's help to give you the haven you need to have this Quiet Time with God. Enlist your spouse to help you find a quiet place. Ask them to assist you with what distracts you while you read. Then return the favor to them. Meet God with as few interferences as possible. After all, you have a meeting with the King of kings. Remove anything that is a distraction so you can focus on Him.

Tip #4: Reduce the quantity of verses you are reading.

I know this sounds unusual coming from a preacher. Allow me to explain. If you are in a season of your life where you are not understanding or getting anything out of your time with God and His Word, maybe you are trying to read too much. Instead of trying the marathon (reading the Bible through every six months), try reading from the Psalms each day.

For a two-year period of my life, I read just the book of Psalms for my devotions. Every month or so, I would read it through. I would read and try to imagine what the Psalmist was going through as I read. I slowed down my reading and got more from it. If it takes you five years to read through the Bible, you are not less of a Christian. Read it at a pace that you can comprehend it and receive something from it.

In the Bonus Section, I included my monthly reading schedule for the Psalms.

Tip #5: Reset your expectations.

What are the expectations you have when you read the Bible? Perhaps I can help reset them for you. When you read the Bible, you should expect at least one of these things to occur. Copy these five expectations to a note card, put it in your Bible or on your reading device. Read them aloud before you read the Bible each day.

God will have something for me that day in His Word. I will look for it.

God will teach me a precept, a principle, or a promise. I will look for them.

God will help me discern a solution to a problem I am pondering. I will look for that solution.

God will strengthen my faith in Him. I will trust Him as a result of what I read today.

God will renew my courage to walk on with Him. I will walk today in the light of what I read.

God will convince me of how dearly I am loved. I will meditate on His love for me and the security of His love.

I encourage you to make your own list of expectations of God. Think about the things that you love to look for about God's character and nature.

Tip #6: Read with a companion.

I would encourage you to have a companion with whom you can seek clarification or get the sense of something. If you do not understand something, how will you learn unless you ask? Do not be afraid to seek help. This companion might be:

A trusted friend--identify someone with whom you are comfortable being spiritually vulnerable. Contact them. Tell them, "I need someone I can call when I am stuck understanding a passage. Will you be my devotional companion?"

A spiritual adviser--your pastor, Sunday School teacher, or a deacon at church may help you as you seek clarification.

A printed Bible reference companion book--a book that helps you understand passages in bite-sized pieces. (See Bonus Section for suggestions.)

A devotional commentary--a trusted author who gives the sense of the passage and teaches a principle or precept from the passage. (See Bonus Section.)

Tip #7: Reflect on your daily reading.

Reading without reflection causes me frustration later in the day. Reflection is pondering the words you read and then looking deeply into your soul and spirit. The time for reflection is the time when you give unrestricted access to God to adjust and remove the elements brought to light from your reading as you reflect on His Word and while the Holy Spirit works on your heart. As you first begin, give yourself thirty seconds for reflection. Work your way up to several minutes for reflecting. I think of it as a time to acknowledge what I read, appreciate what I read, and ask God to change me based on what I read.

Tip #8: Revise your reading plan.

I would not recommend the same Bible reading schedule for every season in your life. (I will put various plans in the Bonus Section.) I sometimes read a plan of ten chapters a day from random books. Other times I read a plan of themes I can choose within my Bible software on my portable devices and computer. There are times I read a devotional book and its assigned reading. Try different plans of Bible reading; the variety will engage your senses and heart.

My goal is to give you the tools to overcome **the Obstacle of Comprehension**. When you get stuck, review these eight tips. If you used this method, and it helped, <u>email</u> me to let me know. My <u>email</u> address is in the Bonus Section.

CHAPTER SEVEN

THE OBSTACLE OF

RECOLLECTION

THE OBSTACLE OF RECOLLECTION

The Obstacle of Recollection--_I wish I could remember my Devotions thirty minutes later. I tried. I failed. It makes me feel the negative emotions of guilt and sadness._

Why is it we can watch a sports event, look at a television program, or even a movie and remember lines, scenes, and emotions from the event? What is it about the events in our lives that make us remember some things clearly and other things not at all? Why is it we can remember our first ice cream cone, first kiss, and first speeding ticket (Hopefully, those three events were not on the same day for you!), and yet, we forget the things we should remember.

This selective memory occurs not only in the secular realm. It happens in the spiritual realm. Why?

I do not hold a degree in any applied science to give you

researched answers on this subject of recollection, but I can tell you what I have seen in my life. The more senses I engage in an event, the more I remember it. Is it this way for you? You can smell an apple pie which takes you back in time to a place, a person, an event, a moment, and a treasured memory with just one smell. Just one sound can transport you to a time in your life that touched you. It only takes a scene you see to open the window of your mind, and you are reminded of a similar life event from a previous decade.

This makes me wonder at times in my Bible reading: how many senses am I deploying when it comes to Bible reading? It may have something to do with the senses we engage when we read the Bible.

The more senses I engage in reading, the more memorable my time with Him will be. In our lives, there are enough things that oppose the Word of God that will seek to rob us of what we read thirty minutes later. I am asking you today to be intentional in your Bible reading to engage your senses.

Jesus spoke of the Word of God as a seed being sown by a sower (Luke 8:5-8). The sower goes out to sow seeds. He casts the same seed on different types of soil. The way Jesus explained it, sometimes the seed hits land that is not ready for growth. He spoke of opponents and obstacles to the seed taking root. Jesus speaks of this to illustrate the Word of God going forth and taking hold in the hearts of men.

I do not like the days when I read and forget what I read thirty minutes later. To me, it is like the birds in the parable Jesus told; they come and take the seed of what I read. Then, as if I needed more guilt to carry around, I end up feeling sorry. I let the seed get snatched from my mind. I was not intentional in my thoughts on His Word.

If this happens, I refer to this axiom: read less to remember more. I discussed in another section of this volume that you can slow down in your reading. While the Bible is an all-you-can-eat buffet, take your time. Select a portion of Scripture and read it to understand it, grasp it, and live it. I would far rather you read the same chapter or passage five days in a row until you get it and live it than to read a whole book in a week and you forget it.

The Word of God is powerful; it is like a sharp sword that exposes what it touches. When the Word of God touches you, you will remember it.

When I want to remember what I read more than thirty minutes from now, I follow these tips to engage my spiritual senses:

Tip #1: Engage the spiritual sense of sight--the physical Bible or digital Bible you use for Devotions.

Growing up, I remember hearing people speaking about knowing where a verse was on the page. They would make marks in their favorite Bible. Some people like to underline or put a distinctive mark on the passage.

If you are comfortable with doing so, make marks in your Bible with pens or highlighters. Use specific colors for specific things. You could use:

Purple--when God is mentioned.

Pink--when women are mentioned.

Red--when love, mercy, grace, and compassion are mentioned.

Green--when spiritual growth is mentioned.

Yellow--when prayer, praise, worship, and heaven are mentioned.

Blue--when commands and instructions are mentioned.

Orange--when history is mentioned.

Grey--when death, sin, hell, and Satan are mentioned.

If you use a digital Bible, you could save your highlights so that they appear in the text. This way of reading your Bible engages your sight which can aid remembering what you read later in the day.

You could also choose, if you are privileged to own more than one Bible, to have a Bible that you use only for reading your Devotions. I prefer a paragraph-based Bible for this type reading if I must use a bound Bible. (Check the Resource Section for the Bible I use for this.)

Tip #2: Engage the spiritual sense of hearing.

Use an audio Bible:

> You could listen to the Bible being read aloud by someone. I know some who holds their Bible open to the passage as the narrator reads it. When you use an audio Bible, it activates three senses: touch, hearing, and sight. Occasionally, I use an audio Bible for my reading to help me connect with His words more. I will also listen to the Bible just for something to listen to while driving, walking, or thinking. I use an audio Bible to help me learn how to pronounce the words. There are excellent recordings of the Bible available. You may have a commute for work and would find this mode of Bible reading helpful.

> Check the Bonus Section for a link to audio Bibles.

Reading aloud:

> You could engage the sense of hearing by reading the

Bible aloud. Select your passage and read it aloud. Reading the Bible aloud helps me stay focused like few other things. Yes, it can be weird to do, but it works. Besides, being normal is over-rated! If you are at home when you read, gather your children and read to them. If you and your spouse are alone, read aloud to each other. If you are in a coffee shop, sit outside and read aloud. Engage the sense of hearing when you read to have a memorable reading time.

Tip #3: Engage the spiritual sense of touch.

Your Bible:

I love the feel of a leather Bible. I love to caress the leather. I like the feel of the Bible's paper. Holding your Bible while you read engages the sense of touch. It is direct contact with God through His preserved words for you. You are in touch with God. Treat it carefully and respectfully.

You may enjoy taking colored pencils and illuminating your Bible with colors. There are resources in the Bonus Section to help you engage the sense of touch.

Your Bible app:

The Bible is God's Word whether it is displayed on a hand-held screen, projected by a projector onto the wall, or on your computer monitor. When you open your Bible app, turn off your notifications if you can and totally engage your mind and hands in the app. You are touching the very words of God. It is not in a museum case or an artifact. It is in your hands; treat it carefully.

Your 3x5 cards:

I love using 3x5 cards. I enjoy writing ideas, tasks, and thoughts on them. When memorizing Scripture, copy verses onto these cards to help you to meditate, learn, and reflect.

Your notebook:

I have a personal project I am working on that involves writing with a fountain pen and paper. I practice my handwriting (which needs practice) by copying Scripture from my Bible to paper. This simple act puts me in touch with God's Word.

Tip #4: Engage the spiritual sense of taste.

Throughout Scripture, God engages the senses through taste. He gave His people manna to taste. He uses the word "*taste*" figuratively to convey the Word of God is like bread, honey, water, and sweetness. Engaging this sense in Bible reading requires intentional thought. It is taking the words you read and savoring their flavor in your life. Sometimes the Word of God is referred to as bitter taste. Develop taste buds for the Word of God and your taste buds for the world will diminish.

Tip #5: Engage the spiritual sense of smell.

God gave us the sense of smell. Have you considered how important smell is to God? He fills His courts with fragrance. Our praise is a fragrance to Him. Our offerings have a scent to Him. Our sacrifices are a fragrance to Him.

When you read His words, do you catch a fragrance of Him? Your reading of His Word brings you into His presence, and this worship has a fragrance that is pleasant to Him.

My goal is to give you the tools to overcome **the Obstacle of Recollection**. When you get stuck, review these five tips. If you used this method, and it helped, email me to let me know. My email address is in the Bonus Section.

CHAPTER EIGHT

THE OBSTACLE OF APPLICATION

THE OBSTACLE OF APPLICATION

The Obstacle of Application--*I do not know how to apply Scripture to my life.*

I know what it is like to struggle with applying Scripture. You begin to feel inadequate and eventually want to stop reading your Bible. You are not alone. I am right there with you; I know this struggle.

Many people from all walks of life and academic backgrounds feel this way or have felt this way. Like you, they read a passage and think, "Okay I understand every English word. But here is my life right now: my kid just punched another kid at school; my income is low; my expenses are high; I have a daughter who is in trouble; a son who is away from God, and I am feeling awfully low. How do I apply my daily reading to my life?"

Do you agree with these statements?

The Bible is academic,

but it is more than a textbook.

The Bible is scientific,

> but it is more than theory.

The Bible is philosophical,

> but it is more than ideas.

The Bible is historical,

> but it is more than a collection of history.

The Bible is chronological,

> but it is more then a timeline of man.

The Bible is literature,

> but it is more than prose and verse.

The Bible is vocal,

> but it is more than a collection of voices; it speaks.

The Bible is the answer to every human need.

You may agree with my statements above, but within you have you respectfully asked these questions:

Why does the Bible not speak to me?

Why can I read the Bible's words, but lack the ability to apply it?

Why is it I understand my relationship with Jesus, but I cannot see how a verse He spoke applies to me?

How is it I can read manuals at work and teach others how to follow the instructions to make a product or fix a device; yet, the very manual for my life I read and just scratch my head?

How is it I can read a recipe or watch a cooking show and go to the kitchen and create what I just learned, but I cannot do that with the Bible?

How is it that a book translated in English at less than a high school diploma level is hard to wrap my mind around and apply? Why?

Applying Scripture to your life is what brings the Word of God to life. It takes you from drifting and wondering to life engaged with the Bible. I love when I get the sense of the verse and can relate it to someone else. I tend to preach and write as I understand a verse or passage of Scripture.

I am a visual thinker and need to see something to understand it. I tend to look for a moment in life to connect the truth of a passage to my life. I want to help you move from obstacles to overcoming. I want what I write to bring you to the intersection of Bible learning and Bible living.

You can learn to apply any passage to your life with three Bible study methods I personally use in my life. Each of the three methods are designed to take you from personal frustration with your Bible reading to a place where applying the Bible comes naturally. I want you to learn to inspect a passage and determine what God is saying to you.

Here are three Bible study methods to help you. They are called the EXAMINE method, the PRAY Method, and the Best Devotions Ever method.

Method One

The EXAMINE Bible Study Method

The EXAMINE Bible study method is what I use when I struggle with applying what I read from the Bible. The word EXAMINE is an acrostic. (An acrostic is a composition where individual letters of a phrase or word begin a sentence.)

This Bible study method is simple and engages both my mind and heart to find the application of a passage as I examine what is there. I developed this method to help me. I hope it helps you.

Read this passage or verse.

"Study to show thyself approved unto God, a workman that needeth not to be ashamed, rightly dividing the word of truth" (2 Timothy 2:15).

Notice the two occupations of the believer. First, there is an indication that the believer is a student in a classroom with a teacher. The second occupation indicated that is the believer is a worker. He or she is in a place of employment with an employer who evaluates the work done. The employee is encouraged to work so as not to be ashamed. The sense of the word "*ashamed*" is to work so as not to be disgraced. The embarrassed or disgraced emotion comes from not completing his assignment.

What is our assignment? Our assignment is to divide the Word of Truth rightly. The phrase, "*rightly divide*" paints a picture of a worker whose assignment is to make a road to a specific destination. The worker would look at the landscape and make a straight line to the other side.

Consider yourself a student in the classroom. You want to apply the Word of God to your life. Your job is to study the Word of God.

Consider yourself a workman or workwoman. You are given a field or forest, and you must make a road to get to the other side in the straightest line possible. There might be pretty sights you want to see along the way, but that is not your assignment. You are to make a straight road for your employer.

The EXAMINE Bible Study method helps us cut a straight road (the Biblical words--"*rightly divide*") through the passage. We do not want to get side tracked with other things until we figure out what does this passage or verse mean and then how does it apply to me?

To examine something means check every detail of something in order to gain some information. This method is more for verse studies than it is for chapter studies. (See Bonus Section for links to download this method and worksheet.)

You may not have an answer for every point of this method. The first time may be hard for you, but push through. If you want, email me or call me, and I will help you through it.

E - **Evaluate** the context of the verse.

Look at the verse in relation to its surrounding verses. What is being said in the five verses before and after? How does the context prepare or conclude the way for the verse you are studying? The sentence you write should start with **The verses before and after are teaching...**

X - **X-Ray** the contents of this passage or verse.

Look intensely at the structure of the verse. (Structure means the phrases, clauses, and marks of punctuation. Does the verse have questions?

OVERCOMING YOUR DEVOTIONAL OBSTACLES

Commands? Principles? Precepts? Promises?) Look at every clause and phrase marked with its punctuation. What do the words mean in their usual definition? What does this passage or verse's meanings say to you? The sentence you write should start with **The structure of this verse contains...**

A - Analyze the passage or verse for any commandments.

Look for any command to obey. A commandment is something we are to do. Look for words like, *say, do, go, be,* or *must.* Ask yourself, "What should I do as a result of reading this passage or verse?" The sentence you write should start with **I will follow God's command to...**

M - Meditate on the comforts in this passage or verse.

List the comforts of this passage or verse. A comfort is something that touches your spirit. It is the emotion tied to the truth presented. What comforts do you find in this passage or verse? The sentence you write should start with **God comforts His children with...**

I - Investigate the cause of this passage or verse.

Why would God choose to include all of the words in

this passage or verse in the Bible? What did someone do or miss in their life that prompted the Holy Spirit to inspire the human author to pen these words? Now, look within your life. Does the same condition apply that prompted the passage or verse to be included in Scripture? The sentence you write should start with **God included this verse to help me to...**

N - Note your convictions from this passage or verse.

By convictions, I mean list what you believe as a result of studying this passage or verse. What is this passage or verse teaching you to do? The sentence you write should start with **Because this verse is in the Bible, I must...**

E - Examine your own comments of this passage or verse.

Review all that you have written about this passage and write a summary sentence. The sentence you write should start with **Today, because I have studied this passage or verse I will...**

Method Two

The PRAY Bible Study Method

Like the EXAMINE Bible study method, the PRAY Bible study method is an acrostic. This Bible study method is simple to complete. It places focus on a short passage. This method engages both the mind and heart to find the application of a passage as you examine what is there. I developed this method to help me. I hope it helps you.

Choose one short passage or a specific verse in which you want to discover its application. I find it difficult to do very many verses. I like to find the paragraph beginning and ending and narrow it down to the verse which I would like to discover its application.

P - Pray. I know it seems obvious to say, but pray!

Ask the Author of the greatest Book of all time to help you discover what He has for you.

Ask Him for wisdom to understand what is preserved for you in His Word.

Ask Him for knowledge to learn what He placed in His Word for you.

Ask Him for His power to discern what He inspired men to write.

Ask Him for His lesson for you from this passage.

R - Read the passage or verse.

Read silently five times.

Read deliberately and pause at every punctuation mark.

Read the passage or verse aloud at least once. Read it to hear it. If you prefer, use an audio Bible to listen to that verse being read.

A - **Ask** yourself these questions:

Who: Who is doing the speaking? Or to whom is the verse addressed?

What: What precept, principle, promise, or practice is being expressed?

When: When is the action in this verse to be taken? Is there a condition or context mentioned?

Where: Are there places mentioned? Make note of what else happened in the same place in Scripture.

Why: Why did the subject of the passage or verse need to hear the message delivered? Why do you need to know what is here?

How: If this was the only thing you ever read in the Bible, how would you change your life because of its message?

Y - **Yield** yourself to Him.

Are you submitted to obey His Word? All of it? Every word of it?

Are you sensitive to the Holy Spirit's conviction in

this passage?

How does this passage call you to draw closer to Him because you read it?

Method Three

Your Best Devotions Ever Bible Study Method

Your Best Devotions Ever Bible study method uses five prompts to help you have the Best Devotions Ever. While the title is ambitious, once you do it a few times, you will see how helpful it is. I began using this method when I was a very young. My father gave me the essence of it. I have modified it over the last forty years. I gave the method a name, but at its core, it is unchanged.

You can use index cards or an index card app. You also could add notes to your digital Bible app or your digital journal app. I encourage you review the index card at least four times in twenty-four hours. Save your cards as you will enjoy them in years to come.

5 Steps to Your Best Devotions Ever

Passage Read:

Date:

Write a simple, deep, or catchy title for this passage.

What is the best phrase or verse that supports your choice for a title?

What verse challenges you the most?

Write out a one sentence prayer that requests God's help for the above challenge.

What can you do today that will show you have applied this passage to your life?

While I can show you steps to take and methods to follow, you will need to develop your own set of skills.

Do not put too much pressure on yourself. Take your time. If it takes you two days to fill out one of the methods, it is fine. Get a win for yourself by completing one method. Try doing one method for a week. Then try one of the other two methods in this section, which are designed to assist with Bible application, for a week. You will gravitate to one more than another.

In the Bonus Section, you will find links to download and print these methods. Each method will have the study guide with explanation and a worksheet version with blanks.

My goal is to give you the tools to overcome **the Obstacle of Application**. When you get stuck, review these three Bible study methods to assist with applying Scripture. If you used these methods, and they helped, <u>email</u> me to let me know. My <u>email</u> address is in the Bonus Section.

CHAPTER NINE

BONUS SECTION

INTRODUCTION

You will find downloadable worksheets, teaching outlines, Bible study methods, and the Bible reading schedule mentioned in this book when you visit omalleybooks.com/store. These resources are in a PDF format.

PRESSING THE SPIRITUAL RESET BUTTON

In obstacle three, the **Obstacle of Comparison,** in **Tip #3 (Reset yourself),** I mentioned the need to reset your spiritual expectations in three areas.

The three areas deal with your own expectations. Below, I amplify this section on having reasonable expectations in three areas. You should have a reasonable expectation in your walk with God, your prayer life, and your Bible reading.

Reset the expectation of your walk with God.

You must start with a reset of your expectations about your walk with God. Your walk with God is the time you spend in His Word listening to Him and your time talking to Him along with how you live what you have heard in the Word of God.

What does your walk with God mean? To answer that question, I want you to think about my wife and me. I want you to think of a picture with me. I am six feet and six inches tall (198.12 cm), my wife is five feet and one inch tall (154.94 cm). Our stature differs as much as our strides differ. We will walk the same distance, we take a different number of steps to cover the same ground. We wear fitness trackers, and hers registers more steps than mine registers for me. My stride differs from Kim's stride. We walk the same trail, cover the same distance, but we conclude our walk with a different number of steps.

We also see things differently. I see things she will not see. Each perspective brings a different experience. I may have walked on that track and Kim has not. I may have climbed a trail she missed. At the end of the journey, we cannot compare our strides; we just know we started together and finished together. We experienced a similar event, but because of who we are, our physical fitness and stamina, we also have a different experience.

It is the same way for Devotions. You will hold the same kind of Bible in your hand as someone else. You can read the same passage as another person does. You can finish reading the passage within moments of each other. Did you share the same event? Yes, you shared the same event (when you both read the same verses), but your experiences differed. Your spiritual life experiences, emotions, ideas, and spiritual fitness are all part of your spiritual stride.

You cannot compare the strides (who read it faster), the distance covered (who read more), nor can you compare the lengths of notes each of you took (what each of you saw on the same path). The Holy Spirit dwells in the heart of each believer. He will impress each reader in the way that they need to hear and learn. Why then would you compare your Bible journey to someone else's Bible journey? You will have a different stride, a different posture, and a different level of energy than someone else.

You must reset your thinking about comparing your devotional life with anyone else. You must begin to ask God, "Am I meeting Your expectations in my walk with You?"

Reset the expectations about the time you pray.

No one of us is alike in life. It is the same in the spiritual sense, especially when it comes to prayer. Pressing the Spiritual Reset Button on prayer helps you determine what level of prayer life you should have. The comparison between another's prayer life and your own will either make you feel pride or pity. Neither emotion is an accurate metric to assess whether you pray enough or if you pray as long and or as eloquent as someone else. Do you recall what occurred in the temple in Luke 18:9-14? The Pharisee and the Publican both prayed to God, but their hearts were different. What is your heart filled with when you pray?

What is prayer? It is the label or title we use to describe a conversation with God. The Divine conversation occurs as I listen to His Word as I read it, and then I speak back to Him in prayer. The conversation can include requests, thanks, and expressing the concerns of the heart. As with any other communication in our lives, there can be pauses in the conversation, especially when you are gathering your thoughts or reviewing the impressions from the passage you read. The conversation must be more than, "God, here is my grocery list. Please fill my cart with these items and pay for them so I can get going." If this is how you experience prayer in your life, it is no wonder you get so overwhelmed when you compare your devotional life with someone else's devotional life.

What should your prayer life look like after you press your Spiritual Reset Button? You will stop evaluating anyone else's conversation with your Father, and you will concern yourself with your own conversations. You will no longer imagine what they are saying to your Father, or how long it took them to say it, or even how long it took for them to hear from God.

Instead, you will dwell on what you are saying to God and what He is saying to you. You will not think about length of the prayer, the lighting in the room, or the posture you maintained. It will be irrelevant to you whether your hands were turned down, turned up, or raised up in the air. You will not be so absorbed with the posture of prayer, whether you are kneeling or standing, the tone and volume of your voice, and how many titles you used for God and how many times you repeated those titles, or if you prayed until someone saw you praying and posted the picture for you.

When you choose to press the Spiritual Reset Button, your prayer life changes, ending the childish comparison of ourselves with others. Your prayer life must not be evaluated by the length of your prayers, the tone of your voice, the volume of your voice, the movement of your hands and arms, the titles you used for God, or how many times we spoke a name for God in our prayer. There should not be a difference in your public prayers and your personal prayers, save for the subjects you cover. Prayer is talking to God about what is in your heart and listening to Him speak through His Word. Do not complicate prayer. Do not compare your prayer time with another. Doing so cheapens your intimate conversations with God and diminishes you.

Reset the expectations about your Bible reading.

It amazes me how overwhelmed, guilty, and inadequate people feel when they obsess over and compare someone else's Bible reading schedule plan and pattern. Yet, they do not apply the same diligence to the frequency of their own devotional life. If you struggle in this area, stop struggling. As I wrote earlier, we are different people with different rates of speed at which we read and comprehend. Focus on one thing about your Bible reading as you overcome the devotional obstacles of guilt, inadequacy, and being overwhelmed in your comparisons to others.

Let your Bible reading be more about what you retain and live out versus how much you read and left out of your life. What does life look like after you press the Spiritual Reset Button? I recommend you start with quality over quantity. If you are using a devotional book, take the passage for the day and read it. Read it slowly and deliberately. Read it aloud, perhaps even listen to it being read with an audio Bible. Then, read the day's reading of inspiration or instruction. Did the passage from the Bible or the day's reading resonate with you? Is there an area of your life you need to make it apply?

Focus less on how much you read and place the focus how much it changed you. I know people who boast of the times they read through the Bible in a year, but it never changed them in their hearts. By all means, read every word in the Bible. Let it change and shape your life. I would rather take five years to read it through once, than to have read it once each year and missed the message of it because I was marking off my to-do list when it came to Bible reading.

If you are prone to comparing your Bible reading and devotional reading time with someone else, stop it. It is not healthy for your spiritual life. It will leave you overwhelmed, guilty, and feeling less than adequate.

EXAMINE BIBLE STUDY METHOD

The EXAMINE Bible study method is what I use when I struggle with applying what I read. The word EXAMINE is an acrostic. (An acrostic is a composition where individual letters of a phrase or word begin a sentence.)

This Bible study method is simple and engages both my mind and heart to find the application of a passage as I examine what is there. I developed this method to help me. I hope it helps you.

Read this passage or verse.

> *"Study to show thyself approved unto God, a workman that needeth not to be ashamed, rightly dividing the word of truth"* (2 Timothy 2:15).

Notice the two occupations of the believer. First, there is an indication the believer is a student in a classroom with a teacher. The second occupation indicated is the believer is a worker. He or she is in a place of employment with an employer who evaluates the work done. The employee is encouraged to work so as not to be ashamed. The sense of the word ashamed is to work so as not to be disgraced. The embarrassed or disgraced emotion comes from not completing his assignment.

So, what is our assignment? Our assignment is to divide the Word of Truth rightly. The phrase, *"rightly divide"* paints a picture of a worker whose assignment is to make a road to a specific destination. The worker would look at the landscape and make a straight line to the other side.

Consider yourself a student in the classroom. You want to apply the Word of God to your life. Your job is to study the Word of God.

Consider yourself a workman or workwoman. You are given a field or forest, and you must make a road to get to the other side in the straightest line possible. There might be pretty sights along the way you want to see, but that is not your assignment. You are to make a straight road for your employer.

The EXAMINE Bible Study method helps us cut a straight road (the Biblical words--*"rightly divide"*) through the passage. We do not want to get sidetracked with other things until we figure out what does this passage or verse mean and then how does it apply to me?

To examine something means check every detail of something in order to gain some information. This method is more for verse studies than it is for chapter studies.

You may not have an answer for every point of this method. The first time may be hard for you, but push through. If you want, email me or call me, and I will help you through it.

E - Evaluate the context of the verse.

- Look at the verse in relation to its surrounding verses.
- What is being said in the five verses before and after?
- How does the context prepare or conclude the way for the verse you are studying?
- The sentence you write should start with **The verses before and after are teaching:**

X - X-Ray the contents of this passage or verse.

- Look intensely at the structure of the verse. (Structure means, the phrases, clauses, and marks of punctuation. Does the verse have questions? Commands? Principles? Precepts? Promises?)
- Look at every clause and phrase marked with its punctuation.

- What do the words mean in their usual definition?

- What does this passage or verse's meanings say to you?

- The sentence you write should start with **The structure of this verse contains...**

3.   **A - Analyze** the passage or verse for any commandments.

- Look for any command to obey.

- A commandment is something to do. Look for words like *say, do, go, be,* or *must.*

- Ask yourself, "What should I do as a result of reading this passage or verse?"

- The sentence you write should start with **I will follow God's command to...**

M - Meditate on the comforts in this passage or verse.

- List the comforts of this passage or verse.

- A comfort is something that touches your spirit. It is the emotion tied to the truth presented.

- What comforts do you find in this passage or verse?

- The sentence you write should start with **God comforts His children with...**

I - Investigate the cause of this passage or verse.

• Why would God choose to include all of the words in this passage or verse in the Bible.

• What did someone do or miss in their life that prompted the Holy Spirit to inspire the human author to pen these words.

• Look within your life. Does the same condition apply that prompted the passage or verse to be included in Scripture?

• The sentence you write should start with **God included this verse to help me to...**

N - Note your convictions from this passage or verse.

• By convictions I mean, list what you believe as a result of studying this passage or verse.

• What is this passage or verse teaching you to do?

• The sentence you write should start with **I believe because this verse is in the Bible I must...**

E - Examine your own comments of this passage or verse.

• Review all that you have written about this passage and write a summary sentence.

• The sentence you write should start with **Today, because I have studied this passage or verse I will...**

Visit omalleybooks.com/store to download this method.

PRAY BIBLE STUDY METHOD

Choose one short passage or a specific verse in which you want to discover its application.

- I find it difficult to do very many verses.
- I like to find the paragraph beginning and ending and narrow it down to the verse I would like to discover its application.

P - Pray: I know it seems obvious to say, but, pray.

- Ask the Author of the greatest Book of all time to help you discover what He has for you.
- Ask Him for wisdom to understand.
- Ask Him for knowledge to learn.
- Ask Him for His power to discern.
- Ask Him for His lesson for you from this passage.

R - Read the passage or verse.

- Read silently five times. Read deliberately and pause at every punctuation mark in your reading.

• Read the passage or verse aloud at least once. Read it to hear it. If you prefer, use an audio Bible to listen to that verse being read.

A - Ask yourself these questions:

• Who: Who is doing the speaking? Or to whom is the verse addressed.

• What: What is a precept, principle, promise, or practice is being expressed?

• When: When is the action in this verse to be taken? Is there a condition or context mentioned.

• Where: Are there places mentioned? Make note of what else happened in the same place in Scripture.

• Why: Why did the subject of the passage or verse need to hear the message delivered? Why do you need to know what is here?

• How: If this was the only thing you ever read in the Bible, how would you change your life because of its message.

Y - Yield to yourself to Him.

• Are you submitted to obey His Word? All of it? Every word of it?

- Are you sensitive to the Holy Spirit's conviction in this passage?
- How does this passage call you to draw closer to Him because you read it?

Visit omalleybooks.com/store to download this method.

THREE BY FIVE STUDY

See Obstacle One for further explanation.

Items needed: You will need a blank 3x5 card. It can be ruled or unruled. I prefer unruled as I do not like any marks on my cards to distract me.

1.   On a 3x5 card, write a Bible verse on which you want to focus.

   •   Write it neatly and deliberately. Add the punctuation marks.

   • Meditate as you write the words.

   • Sometimes I imagine I am a scribe copying the Word of God from parchment to parchment. It helps me focus and keeps me interested.

2.   Write down these three words:

   • *Inspires:*

   • *Instructs:*

   • *Includes:*

3. Ask yourself these three questions:
    - What **inspires** me in this verse?
    - What **instructs** me in this verse?
    - How am I **included** in this verse?

4. Start each sentence with:
    - This verse inspires me to...
    - This verse instructs me to ...
    - This verse includes me because ... or I am included in this verse because...

Visit <u>omalleybooks.com/store</u> to download this method.

OVERCOMING YOUR DEVOTIONAL OBSTACLES

CONDUCT A TIME INVENTORY

See Obstacle Four Tip Two

Worksheet for Tip #2: Take a simple inventory of where you spend your time.

How many hours do you sleep?

How many hours do you work?

How many hours do you spend in exercise?

How many hours do you spend in leisure?

How many minutes do you spend with God?

Consider how much time you should spend with God this week. Next month, evaluate yourself again. Set a goal to spend ten percent more time with God than you did last month.

Visit omalleybooks.com/store to download this method.

PSALM READING SCHEDULE

This is the Book of Psalms Bible reading method mentioned in Tip Four in the Obstacle Five section.

Day of Month	Chapters
1	1-5
2	6-10
3	11-16
4	17-20
5	21-25
6	26-30
7	31-35
8	36-41
9	42-46
10	47-51
11	52-56
12	57-61
13	62-67
14	68-72

15	73-77
16	78-82
17	83-87
18	88-92
19	93-97
20	98-102
21	103-107
22	108-112
23	113-118
24	119
25	120-125
26	126-130
27	131-136
28	137-140
29	141-144
30	145-147
31	148-150

Visit omalleybooks.com/store to download this schedule.

FIVE STEPS TO YOUR BEST DEVOTIONS EVER

Five Steps to Your Best Devotions Ever

Passage Read:

Date:

Write a simple, deep, or catchy title for this passage.

What is the best phrase or verse that supports your choice for a title?

What verse challenges you the most?

Write out a one sentence prayer that requests God's help for the above challenge.

What can you do today that will show you have applied this passage to your life?

Visit omalleybooks.com/store to download this worksheet.

LINKS TO RESOURCES

Resources Mentioned Throughout the Book

Printed Bibles
- Paragraph Bible
- Cambridge Bibles
- Allen Bibles
- Bible Software
- Life Application Study Bible

Audio Bibles:
- Audio Bible - MP3
- Dramatized Audio Bible
- Audio Bible

Digital Bibles and Software:
- Olive Tree Bible Software
- Faithlife Study Bible Software
- Accordance Bible Software
- ESword

Logos Bible Software

Life Application Bible

Reading Plans and Bible Study Downloads

PDF version for printable worksheets

Dr. Grant Horner's Reading plan

Psalms Reading Plan

Common reading plans

Link to Online Bibles

Blue Letter Bible

Bible Gateway

Tools to Use:

Physical Note Cards

Digital Journal Mac

Digital Journal iOS

Note Card Apps for iOS

Notecards App

Index Card App

Single Commentaries:

The Teacher's Commentary

Old Testament Bible Knowledge Commentary

New Testament Bible Knowledge Commentary

Summarized Bible Companion:

Mentioned in the section The Obstacle of Comprehension, Tip Six

The Summarized Bible Keith Brooks

Resources to Download from omalleybooks.com/store

EXAMINE Bible Study Method

EXAMINE Bible Study Method - Worksheet

PRAY Bible Study Method

PRAY Bible Study Method - Worksheet

Three by Five Bible Study Method

Three by Five Bible Study Method - Worksheet

Time Inventory Worksheet

Psalm Monthly Bible Reading Schedule

Five Steps to your Best Devotions Ever

Outlines for Teachers

MUSIC I LISTEN TO AS I READ AND WRITE

Music I Listen to as I Read and Write

Ocean Sounds

More Ocean Sounds

111 Baroque Classics

RECOMMENDED BOOKS

Devotion Books I Read

Devotional Books:

Spurgeon's Morning and Evening

My Utmost for His Highest

Books on Prayer:

EM Bounds:

The Complete Works of EM Bounds:

Andrew Murray:

With Christ in the School of Prayer

The Collected Works on Prayer

Spiritual Growth Books:

Brother Lawrence:

The Practice of the Presence of God

A. W. Tozer:

The Pursuit of God

Henry Blackaby:

Experiencing God

COMING SOON

Please <u>visit this link to sign-up</u> for early and exclusive access with discounts to publications being released on <u>OMalleyBooks.com</u>

Look for these titles from the *Reflections* Series coming soon:

Reflections From... The *Reflections From* series are written in an expositional-devotional genre.

- *Reflections From Psalm 100*
- *Reflections From the Old Testament: Volumes I and II*
- *Reflections From the New Testament: Volumes I and II*
- *Refections From Ruth: Volumes I-IV*

Reflections on... series are works that are topical, thematic, and instructional.

- *Reflections on Being a Disciple:* This book deals with what Jesus stated it would take to become His disciples.
- *Reflections on God's Mission:* This book identifies

God's mission and answers these questions: Am I to fit God's mission into my life? Or am I to fit my life into His mission?

- *Servant University:* Servant University is my fifteen-week course which teaches the Biblical model of becoming a servant. This course includes a teacher's manual, student workbook, and student daily devotional books that reinforce the lesson to be taught the next Sunday. It is available as a package or individual components. It can be used as a Bible curriculum for homeschools and Sunday Schools. It can be used individually for self-instruction.

43061364R00072

Made in the USA
Middletown, DE
29 April 2017